THE MIXTAPE OF MY LIFE

A DO-IT-YOURSELF MUSIC MEMOIR

ROBERT K. ELDER
ILLUSTRATIONS BY ROB MARVIN

RUNNING PRESS
PHILADELPHIA

Running Press
Hachette Book Group
1290 Avenue of the Americas, New York, NY 10104
www.runningpress.com
@Running_Press

Printed in the United States of America

Published by Running Press, an imprint of Perseus Books, LLC,
a subsidiary of Hachette Book Group, Inc.
The Running Press name and logo is a trademark of the Hachette Book Group.

The publisher is not responsible for websites
(or their content) that are not owned by the publisher.

Print book cover design by Amanda Richmond

Library of Congress Control Number: 2017960254

ISBN: 978-0-7624-6407-4 (paperback)

LSC-C

10 9 8 7 6 5 4 3 2 1

For my wife, Betsy, who introduced me to
Neko Case, the Stylistics, and Parliament-
Funkadelic. I love you and I like your style.
—R.K.E.

For Chelle, who kept the ship afloat
while I was below deck doodling.
—R.M.

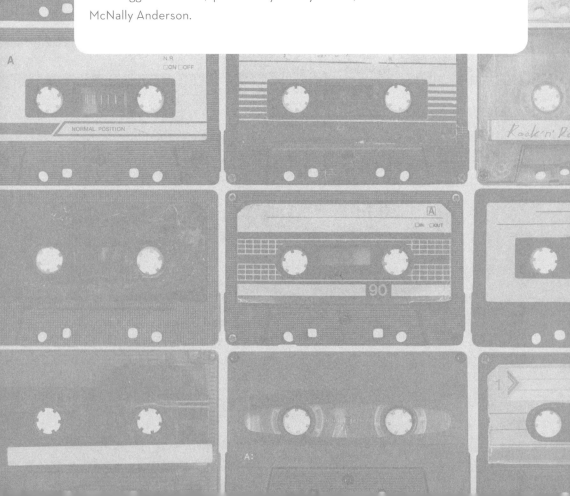

ACKNOWLEDGMENTS

Rob and Rob would like to thank our editor, the amazing Jennifer Kasius, and our indomitable agent David Dunton, who championed this project from the start. Our hats are off to Amanda Richmond, whose design mojo helped bring this book to life. We'd also like to thank Julian Yik Tsao (Yi Cao) for his assistance in setting up the website, populating our Twitter feed and being one of the first sets of eyes to edit the manuscript. Betsy Edgerton and Shannon Zaid also provided invaluable feedback that helped shape the voice of this journal. Lastly, thanks to all of our friends (in person and on social media) who suggested titles, particularly Becky Hume, Michael Bivona and Anne McNally Anderson.

INTRODUCTION

It's said that smell is the sense that most strongly evokes memory.

For me, that's never been true. It's always been hearing music. Music is the key to the time machine in my brain. A song I haven't heard in years can unlock a memory or a sensation I'd long forgotten.

Case in point: I was driving down a Kentucky highway recently and a spin across the radio dial conjured Johnny Lee's "Cherokee Fiddle"—a song I'd almost completely erased from my mind. It was a favorite of my hell-raising, party-loving older cousin Mary Jo, a high school basketball star who died too young. Remembering her love for life and her love for this song was overwhelming.

The Squirrel Nut Zippers' calypso-inspired single "Hell" can still rocket me back to a trip I took to Mendocino County, California, after a bad breakup. My friend Suzanna and her family took me in and we danced all night at a seaside bar, where Groucho Marx's grandson served us drinks. I strongly recommend such an experience for anyone with a broken heart.

Simon and Garfunkel's "Cecilia" was a favorite selection for my wife Betsy's kitchen dance parties when our twins were young. She would holler "MAKING FRIENDS" over the "making love" portion of the verse, to deflect awkward questions. This Puritanical censorship made our friend Sasha explode into laughter.

That's what this book and these questions are designed to do: spark stories, details, and more memories. It is, in essence, a tool to help you write your autobiography and tell personal stories through your music collection. It's not about creating lists of songs, but rather cataloging stories from the soundtrack of your life.

So, enjoy! And be sure to share your stories with us online at Mixtapeofmylife.com and via Twitter at @mixtapemylife.

—Robert K. Elder
Chicagoland, 2018

››› What songs did your parents sing to you in the crib? If you don't know, ask.

Where did they learn these songs?

Create your perfect lullaby playlist,
for yourself or your kids.

....
....
....
....
....
....
....
....
....
....
....
....
....
....
....
....
....
....
....

WHAT ALBUMS OR SONGS DID YOUR PARENTS PLAY AROUND THE HOUSE?

DO YOU KNOW YOUR MOTHER'S FAVORITE SONG AND WHY? IF NOT, ASK HER.

....

....

....

....

....

....

....

SAME QUESTION FOR YOUR FATHER, BROTHER, SISTER, AND GRANDPARENTS.

....

....

....

....

....

....

....

....

....

....

WAS THERE ANY MUSIC
FORBIDDEN IN YOUR HOME?
WHAT WAS IT AND WHY?

....

....

....

....

....

....

....

....

....

....

....

....

....

....

....

....

....

....

....

WHAT WAS THE FIRST SONG
YOU HEARD THAT HAD CURSE WORDS IN IT?
WHO PLAYED IT FOR YOU?

....

....

....

....

....

....

....

....

....

....

....

....

....

....

....

....

....

What song did you realize later was smutty?
When and how? Tell the story.

What artist's appearance surprised you when you saw them for the first time? What were you expecting?

....
....
....
....
....
....
....
....
....
....
....
....
....
....
....
....
....
....
....

WHAT SONG LYRICS FROM GRADE SCHOOL DO YOU REMEMBER? WRITE THEM HERE.

....
....
....
....
....
....
....
....
....
....
....
....
....
....
....
....
....

NOW, LOOK THEM UP ONLINE.
CORRECT THE LYRICS WITH A RED PEN.

WHAT WAS THE FIRST ALBUM YOU OWNED?

....

....

....

....

....

WHO BOUGHT IT FOR YOU?
WHAT WAS THE OCCASION?

....

....

....

....

....

WHAT WAS THE FIRST RECORD
YOU BOUGHT FOR YOURSELF? WHY?

....

....

....

....

....

WHAT BAND DID YOU LOVE IN HIGH SCHOOL THAT EMBARRASSES YOU TODAY? WHY?

WHAT SONG MAKES YOU DANCE
AROUND IN YOUR UNDERWEAR?

Who was your first musical crush?

Did you express it with posters in your locker?
Sketches in your notebook?

....
....
....
....
....
....
....
....
....
....
....
....
....
....
....
....
....
....
....
....

WHAT BANDS' OR ARTISTS' POSTERS DECORATED THE WALLS OF YOUR ROOM?

....

....

....

....

....

....

....

WHERE DID YOU BUY THE POSTERS?

....

....

....

....

....

....

....

....

....

....

DID YOU EVER MEET ONE OF YOUR
FAVORITE ARTISTS?
OR GET AN AUTOGRAPH OR PHOTO?
TELL THE STORY.

PASTE AUTOGRAPH HERE.

WHAT WAS YOUR FIRST CONCERT-GOING EXPERIENCE LIKE? WHO WENT WITH YOU?

....

....

....

....

....

....

....

....

....

....

....

....

....

....

....

....

....

WHAT'S A CONCERT YOU'D LIKE TO RELIVE? CAN YOU RE-CREATE THE SET LIST?

....
....
....
....
....
....
....
....
....
....
....
....
....
....
....
....
....
....
....
....

WHAT'S THE SINGLE BEST CONCERT YOU'VE BEEN TO?

....

WHEN AND WHY?

....

....

....

....

....

....

....

WHAT WAS THE SINGLE MOST DISASTROUS CONCERT?

....

WHEN AND WHY?

....

....

....

....

....

....

....

....

....

....

....

....

....

Make up album names for:

YOUR TEEN YEARS

(Example: Freshman year could be "Lonely Appetite for Destruction.") Have fun, be descriptive and connect each title to what was happening in your life at that time.

13 ....

14 ....

15 ....

16 ....

17 ....

18 ....

19 ....

YOUR COLLEGE YEARS

1 ....

2 ....

3 ....

4 ....

5 ....

THE LAST FEW YEARS

1 ....

2 ....

3 ....

4 ....

WHAT'S THE FIRST
MUSIC VIDEO
YOU REMEMBER? WHERE
AND WHEN DID YOU SEE IT?

WHO GAVE YOU YOUR FIRST MIXTAPE, MIX CD, OR PLAYLIST? DID IT LEAD TO ROMANCE?

....

....

....

....

....

....

....

....

....

....

....

....

TO WHOM DID YOU GIVE YOUR
FIRST MIXTAPE OR PLAYLIST?

....

....

....

HOW DID IT GO?

....

....

....

WHAT SONGS WERE ON IT?

....

....

....

....

....

....

....

WHAT SONG DID YOU SLOW DANCE TO IN JUNIOR HIGH? HIGH SCHOOL? WHO WITH?

....

....

....

....

....

....

....

....

....

....

....

....

....

....

....

....

What music is on your perfect
make-out list? Explain your choices.

....
....
....
....
....
....
....
....
....
....
....
....
....
....
....
....
....
....

WHAT SONGS DO YOU IDENTIFY
WITH YOUR FIRST LOVE AND WHY?

NAME THE SONG THAT HELPED YOU THROUGH A BREAKUP. HOW DID IT HELP?

....

....

....

....

....

....

....

....

....

....

....

....

....

....

....

....

....

....

....

WHICH ARTIST TAUGHT YOU
THE MOST ABOUT LOVE? HOW?

....
....
....
....
....

WHICH ARTIST MISLED YOU ABOUT LOVE? HOW?

....

....

....

....

....

NAME THE SONGS, ALBUMS, OR ARTISTS THAT YOU CAN'T LISTEN TO ANYMORE BECAUSE OF PAST ROMANCES. WHY?

>>> List your ex-partners and the song you most associate with them.

NAME	SONG
....	....
....	....
....	....
....	....
....	....
....	....
....	....
....	....
....	....
....	....
....	....
....	....
....	....
....	....
....	....
....	....
....	....
....	....

What songs were played at your high school graduation ceremony and after party?

....

....

....

....

....

....

....

....

....

....

....

....

....

....

....

....

....

....

KARAOKE TIME:
WHAT'S YOUR GO-TO SONG?

....
....
....
....
....
....
....

WHAT SONG WAS A KARAOKE DISASTER?

....
....
....
....
....
....
....
....
....
....
....

WHAT'S YOUR PERFECT
WORKOUT PLAYLIST?
WHAT SONGS GET YOU
MOTIVATED AND WHY?

....
....
....
....
....
....
....
....
....
....
....
....
....

IS THERE SOMEONE IN YOUR FAMILY
WHO LOVES BROADWAY MUSICALS?
DID YOU SHARE THAT LOVE AND WHAT
WERE YOUR FAVORITE SHOWS AND SONGS?

....

....

....

....

....

....

....

....

....

....

....

....

....

....

....

....

....

WHAT SONGS STICK WITH YOU NOW? WHY?

....

....

....

....

....

....

....

....

SAME QUESTION, BUT FOR OPERA AND JAZZ.

....

....

....

....

....

....

....

....

....

....

>>> **What was your exposure to opera, besides Bugs Bunny's "What's Opera, Doc?"**
(You know: "Kill the Wabbit! Kill the Wabbit!")

....
....
....
....
....
....
....
....
....
....
....
....
....
....
....
....
....
....

What about Disney movie music?
What song carries the most memories?

LIST TV THEME SONGS YOU
KNOW THE WORDS TO. WHAT'S YOUR
FAVORITE AND WHY? WHAT ARE YOUR
ASSOCIATIONS TO THOSE THEMES?

WHAT SONG, WITHOUT FAIL,
MAKES YOU TEAR UP?

....

WHY?

....

....

....

....

....

....

....

....

....

....

....

....

....

....

....

....

LOOK UP THE #1 HITS FOR EACH OF THE YEARS YOU
WERE IN JUNIOR HIGH, HIGH SCHOOL, AND COLLEGE. WRITE
DOWN THE FIRST ASSOCIATION ATTACHED TO EACH SONG.

YEAR	SONG	ASSOCIATION

WHAT ARTISTS INSPIRED YOU TO ADOPT (IN HINDSIGHT) THE MOST HUMILIATING OUTFIT/HAIRCUT? DESCRIBE.

....
....
....
....
....
....
....

WHICH MUSIC TREND OR ARTIST INFLUENCED YOUR OVERALL FASHION SENSE?

....
....
....
....
....
....

>>> **Did you play an instrument or sing in choir in high school? Who sat to your right?**

....

....

....

....

....

....

....

Tell the story of a band or orchestra adventure or road trip.

....

....

....

....

....

....

....

....

Which compositions were your
favorite and why?

....

....

....

....

....

....

....

....

Did you have a solo? For which song or composition?
How did you prepare?

....

....

....

....

....

....

....

....

....

DID YOU SING SONGS ON FAMILY ROAD TRIPS? WHAT WERE THEY?

....

....

....

....

....

....

....

....

....

....

....

....

....

....

....

....

....

....

....

WHAT ALBUMS DO YOU HAVE MULTIPLE COPIES OF, IN DIFFERENT FORMATS?

....
....
....
....
....
....
....
....

WHICH ALBUM ARE YOU MOST LIKELY TO GIVE AS A GIFT? WHY?

....
....
....
....
....
....
....
....
....
....

IS THERE A SONG THAT, WHEN YOU FIND SOMEONE ELSE
WHO LIKES IT, GUARANTEES INSTANT FRIENDSHIP?
WHAT IS IT AND WHAT IS ITS MAGIC?

....

....

....

....

....

....

....

....

....

....

....

....

....

....

....

....

....

....

WHAT RADIO STATIONS DID YOU LISTEN TO GROWING UP?

....
....
....
....
....
....
....
....

WHAT WAS THE FORMAT?

....
....
....
....
....
....
....
....
....
....
....

....
....
....
....
....
....
....

Did you ever win a radio call-in contest?
Tell the story.

....
....
....
....
....
....
....
....
....
....

Did you ever get the lyrics wrong to a favorite song?
When you learned the correct lyrics, how did it
change the meaning?

....
....
....
....
....
....
....
....
....
....
....
....
....
....
....
....
....
....
....

DESERT ISLAND DISCS:
NAME 5 ARTISTS OR ALBUMS
YOU'D HAVE FOR AN EXTENDED STAY.

1. ....

2. ....

3. ....

4. ....

5. ....

CAN YOU SING ANY SONGS IN A DIFFERENT LANGUAGE BESIDE "FRÈRE JACQUES"?

....
....
....
....

WHO TAUGHT THEM TO YOU AND WHY?

....
....
....
....

WHAT DO THE TRANSLATED LYRICS MEAN?

....
....
....
....
....
....
....
....

WHAT'S THE AD JINGLE THAT YOU JUST CAN'T SHAKE? WRITE IT OUT.

Create the perfect road trip playlist.

Annotate your list with comments explaining why you included each track.

....
....
....
....
....
....
....
....
....
....
....
....
....
....
....
....

....

....

....

....

....

....

....

....

....

....

....

....

....

....

....

....

....

....

....

NAME THE BEST NIGHTTIME DRIVING SONG THAT'S NOT "I'M ON FIRE" BY BRUCE SPRINGSTEEN.

....

....

....

....

....

DEFEND YOUR CHOICE.

....

....

....

....

....

....

....

....

....

....

....

....

....

MAKE A PIE CHART.
INCLUDE YOUR SIX FAVORITE ARTISTS, SIZED BY YOUR AFFECTION FOR THEM.

WHO IS A POPULAR ARTIST WHOSE
ALLURE YOU DON'T UNDERSTAND?

....

NOW, ASK A FRIEND WHO IS A FAN TO EXPLAIN
WHAT THEY LIKE ABOUT THE ARTIST AND HAVE
THEM RECOMMEND THREE SONGS YOU MIGHT LIKE.

....

....

....

SO, HOW DID IT GO?

....

....

....

....

....

....

....

....

....

....

WHAT SONGS WERE MUSICAL GATEWAY DRUGS THAT OPENED YOU UP TO A NEW ARTIST OR GENRE?

>>> What song did you think meant one thing, only later to discover it meant something else?

....

....

....

....

....

....

....

....

....

....

....

....

....

....

....

....

....

....

....

List your favorite drinking songs.
Tell the story attached to them.

SONG

STORY

....

....

....

....

....

....

....

....

....

....

....

....

....

....

....

....

....

....

....

....

>>> Name five songs that make you instantly turn off the radio. List reasons why.

SONG   REASONS

....
                             ....
                             ....

....
                             ....
                             ....

....
                             ....
                             ....

....
                             ....
                             ....

....
                             ....
                             ....

What's the best song to put on during a rainy day?

....

Why?

....
....
....
....
....
....
....
....
....
....
....
....
....
....
....
....
....

NAME THE ARTIST WHO YOU OWN THE MOST ALBUMS FROM.

....
....
....

WHY?

....
....
....
....
....
....
....
....
....

WHO IS YOUR FAVORITE SINGER/SONGWRITER? WHY?

....

....

....

....

....

....

....

....

....

....

....

....

....

....

....

....

....

....

....

....

....

....

....

....

....

....

....

....

....

....

....

....

....

....

....

....

....

Does your name appear in any songs?
List them and record your memories.

....
....
....
....
....
....
....
....
....
....
....
....
....
....
....
....
....
....
....
....

WHAT ARE YOUR FAVORITE SILLY/NONSENSICAL SONGS?

....

....

....

....

....

....

....

....

....

....

....

....

....

....

....

....

....

....

WHAT SONGS CALM YOU
WHEN YOU'RE FEELING ANXIOUS?

....

....

....

....

....

....

....

....

....

....

....

....

....

....

....

....

....

....

....

Lounge Music Vol. 1

A160

WHO WROTE YOUR FAVORITE SONG? IF YOU DON'T KNOW, LOOK IT UP.

....

WHAT OTHER SONGS DID THEY WRITE?

....
....
....
....
....
....
....
....
....
....
....
....
....
....
....
....

DID THIS PERSON WRITE FOR OTHER ARTISTS?

....

DID THEY WRITE OTHER SONGS THAT
EVOKE SPECIFIC MEMORIES?

....
....
....
....
....
....
....
....
....
....
....
....
....
....
....
....
....
....

>>> Who directed the music video that had the most impact on you? Why?

What other videos or movies did this director
make that affected you?

WHAT ARTIST IS
A GUILTY PLEASURE?

....
....
....
....
....

WHY? RECORD A MEMORY
THAT ILLUSTRATES YOUR POINT.

....
....
....
....
....
....
....
....

WHAT IS YOUR FAVORITE
MOVIE SOUNDTRACK
AND WHY?

....

....

....

....

....

....

....

....

....

....

....

....

....

....

....

....

....

....

WHAT MUSICAL LYRIC IS MEANINGFUL
ENOUGH THAT YOU MIGHT CONSIDER A TATTOO?
OR MAYBE A FULL PAGE IN THIS JOURNAL.

DRAW A DESIGN FOR IT.

SONG

MEMORIES

....

....
....
....

....

....
....
....

....

....
....
....

....

....
....
....

List your most memorable family vacations and the songs you associate with them. Why?

SONG

VACATIONS

....
....
....
....
....
....
....
....
....
....
....
....
....
....
....
....
....

WERE YOU EVER IN A BAND OUTSIDE OF SCHOOL?

....
....
....
....
....
....

AND WHAT WERE YOUR SONGS LIKE? COVERS? ORIGINALS? LIST SOME SONG TITLES.

....
....
....
....
....
....
....
....
....
....
....
....

WHICH PERFORMANCES WERE THE MOST MEMORABLE?

....
....
....
....
....
....

WHERE ARE THE OTHER BAND MEMBERS NOW?

....
....
....
....
....
....
....
....
....
....
....
....

WHAT SONG DO YOU FIND EMBARRASSINGLY EARNEST?

....

AND WHY DO YOU IDENTIFY WITH IT?

....

....

....

....

....

....

....

WHAT SONGS HAVE EXPANDED YOUR VOCABULARY?

....

....

....

....

....

....

....

....

....

....

....

....

....

....

....

....

....

....

....

....

....

....

Circle the words these songs have in common.
What does that say about you?

1. ....

2. ....

3. ....

4. ....

5. ....

6. ....

7. ....

8. ....

9. ....

10. ....

WHAT ARE YOUR FAVORITE
HOLIDAY SONGS?

....

WHY?

....
....
....
....
....
....
....

WHAT'S YOUR LEAST FAVORITE HOLIDAY SONG?

....

ALSO, WHY?

....

....

....

....

....

....

....

DID YOU EVER USE A SONG
TO APOLOGIZE? TELL THE STORY.

....

....

....

....

....

....

....

....

....

....

....

....

....

....

....

....

....

....

DID YOU EVER USE A SONG
TO MAKE A POINT? EXPLAIN.

>>> Name some songs whose meanings have changed for you. What did they first mean, what do they mean now and what changed your impressions? How do you understand them differently?

....

....

....

....

....

....

....

....

....

....

....

....

....

....

....

....

CREATE CALL LETTERS AND A STATION ID FOR A STATION THAT ONLY PLAYS MUSIC THAT YOU LIKE.

DRAW THE STATION LOGO.

ALBUM TRACKS VS. SINGLES: WHAT ARE YOUR FAVORITE SONGS THAT NEVER MADE IT TO RADIO?

....

....

....

....

....

....

....

WHAT MEMORIES ARE ATTACHED TO THEM?

....

....

....

....

....

....

....

....

....

....

SAME QUESTION, BUT APPLY THIS TO B-SIDES, IMPORTS, AND LIVE VERSIONS OF SONGS.

....

....

....

....

....

....

....

....

....

....

....

....

....

....

....

....

....

....

Word Association Game

Write the songs you associate with these words, and why:

FIRE ....

....

RAIN ....

....

COOL ....

....

WINTER ....

....

HIP ....

....

CHILD ....

....

SMOKE ....

....

DANGER ....

....

SWEET ....

....

SULTRY ....

....

SAD ....

....

HUNGRY ....

....

WHITE SNAKE ....

....

WHAT SONG LYRIC DIDN'T YOU UNDERSTAND UNTIL YEARS LATER?

....

....

....

....

....

....

....

....

....

....

....

....

....

....

....

....

....

....

....

....

SPORTS SONGS:
WHAT SONGS DO YOU ASSOCIATE
WITH GAMES/TEAMS, AND WHY?

WHAT'S YOUR FAVORITE USE
OF DOUBLE ENTENDRE IN A SONG?

(Think "Milkshake" by Kelis or
Aerosmith's cover of "Big Ten Inch Record.")

HAS YOUR OPINION ABOUT A SONG OR AN
ARTIST EVER CAUSED A FIGHT? WHAT HAPPENED?

....

....

....

....

....

....

....

....

....

....

....

....

....

....

....

....

....

....

....

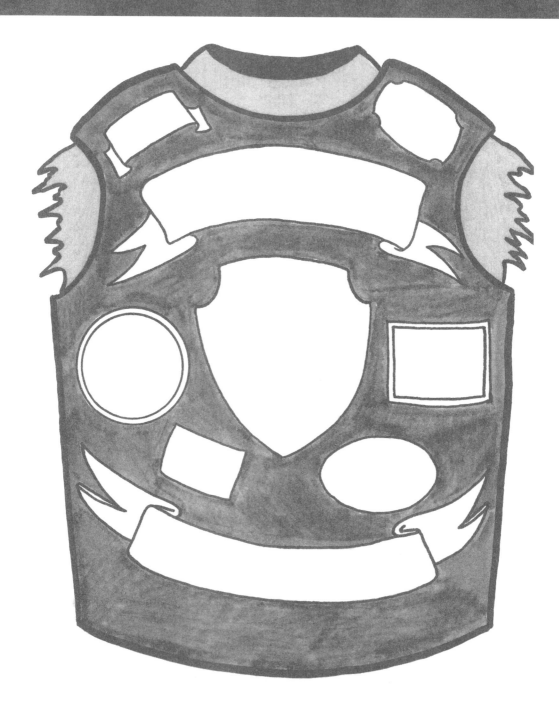

What songs are cautionary tales that you've taken advice from? (Examples: "Cat's in the Cradle" or "Don't be Cruel.") How did you apply them to your life?

....

....

....

....

....

....

....

....

....

....

....

....

....

....

....

....

....

....

WHAT ARE THE MOST POWERFUL
SONGS ABOUT WAR OR CONFLICT?

....

....

....

....

....

....

....

....

....

....

....

....

....

....

....

....

....

....

WHAT ARE THE BEST
SONGS ABOUT PEACE? WHY?

....

....

....

....

....

....

....

....

....

....

....

....

....

....

....

....

....

....

....

WHAT ARE YOUR FAVORITE SONGS OF THE SUMMER?
ATTACH A YEAR AND SPECIFIC MEMORY TO THEM.

YEAR	SONG	MEMORIES
....	....	....
....	....	....
....	....	....
....	....	....
....	....	....
....	....	....
....	....	....
....	....	....
....	....	....
....	....	....
....	....	....
....	....	....
....	....	....
....	....	....
....	....	....
....	....	....
....	....	....
....	....	....

>>> What band do you want to like, but they never quite
hooked you? Why?

....

....

....

....

....

....

....

....

....

....

....

....

....

....

....

....

....

....

WHO TAUGHT YOU TO DANCE
AND WHAT WERE THE SONGS?

WHAT SONGS DO YOU REQUEST
FOR DANCING AT PARTIES?

WHAT'S THE SCARIEST ALBUM COVER?
DRAW IT AND EXPLAIN WHY.

....

....

....

....

....

....

....

....

....

....

....

....

....

....

....

....

....

....

....

....

....
....
....
....
....
....
....
....
....
....
....
....
....
....
....
....
....

What song or artist makes you laugh? Explain.

SOMETIMES, YOU HEAR A SNIPPET OF A SONG
BUT CAN'T IDENTIFY IT FOR YEARS.
WHAT WAS YOUR LONGEST HUNT FOR
A SONG AND HOW DID YOU RESOLVE IT?

THE FINEST WORK SONGS:
CREATE THE BEST PLAYLIST
TO DO HOUSEHOLD CHORES TO.

ASSIGN SONG TITLES TO
EACH OF YOUR EX-LOVES

Examples: Led Zeppelin's "Heartbreaker" or Taylor Swift's "Bad Blood"—
songs that best describe your relationship. Quote the relevant passages;
explain why the titles are apt.

....

....

....

....

....

....

....

....

....

....

....

....

....

....

....

....

....

WHAT SONGS SOUND THE BEST COMING OUT OF HEADPHONES? GIVE YOUR RATIONALE AND PERSONAL TESTIMONY.

WHAT SONGS SOUND THE BEST COMING OUT OF HOME SPEAKERS?

....
....
....
....
....
....
....
....
....
....
....
....
....
....
....
....
....
....
....
....

WHAT'S THE BEST MOVIE THEME SONG AND WHAT MEMORY DO YOU HAVE ATTACHED TO IT?

....

....

....

....

....

....

....

....

....

....

....

....

....

....

....

....

....

....

WHAT SONG OR ARTIST MAKES
YOU FALL ASLEEP? WHY?

....
....
....
....
....
....
....
....
....
....
....
....
....
....
....
....
....
....
....
....
....
....

....

....

....

....

....

....

....

....

....

....

....

....

....

....

....

....

....

....

....

....

....

What is the song or album that you can't believe you once liked? Why are you disenchanted now?

....

....

....

....

....

....

....

....

....

....

....

....

....

....

....

....

....

....

....

SONGS THAT HELP YOU STAY COOL.

SONGS THAT KEEP YOU WARM.

WHAT ARE YOUR FAVORITE PARODY SONGS?
AND WHERE DID YOU LEARN / HEAR THEM?

....

....

....

....

....

....

....

....

....

....

....

....

....

....

....

....

....

....

WRITE YOUR OWN PARODY LYRICS, USING
THE STRUCTURE OF YOUR FAVORITE SONG.

>>> Time travel: Which songs have the ability to instantly take you to a specific time and place? Please expound.

WHAT ARE YOUR
MUSICAL 10 COMMANDMENTS,
WISDOM FROM SONGS
THAT ARE WORDS TO LIVE BY?

(Example: "You Can't Always Get What You Want" by the Rolling Stones.)

1. ....

2. ....

3. ....

4. ....

5. ....

6. ....

7. ....

8. ....

9. ....

10. ....

WHERE DID YOU WEAR IT?

....

....

....

....

....

....

DID IT HELP YOU MAKE NEW FRIENDS?

....

....

....

....

....

....

WHERE IS IT NOW?

....

....

....

....

....

....

>>> Create your perfect playlist for a night of
romantic entanglement:

....

....

....

....

....

....

....

....

....

....

....

....

....

....

....

....

....

....

....

....

....

What song makes you automatically happy?

....

Why?

....

....

....

....

....

....

....

....

....

....

....

....

....

....

....

....

....

....

THE 5 SENSES,

A FREE ASSOCIATION GAME.
WRITE THE FIRST SONG TITLE THAT COMES
TO MIND FOR THE FOLLOWING SENSES:

SIGHT ....

SOUND...

SMELL ....

TOUCH...

TASTE ....

CREATE YOUR PERFECT
WEDDING RECEPTION PLAYLIST.
WHAT DOES IT SAY ABOUT YOU?

....

....

....

....

....

....

....

....

....

....

....

....

....

....

....

....

....

....

....

What song plays in your head as you cinematically saunter down the street?

(Examples: "Stayin' Alive" from *Saturday Night Fever* or "Little Green Bag" from *Reservoir Dogs*.)

....

....

....

....

....

....

....

....

....

....

....

....

....

....

....

....

....

....

Did you ever wait in line to buy an album?
Who was the artist and why?

....

....

....

....

....

....

....

....

....

....

....

DRAW YOUR FAVORITE ALBUM COVER:

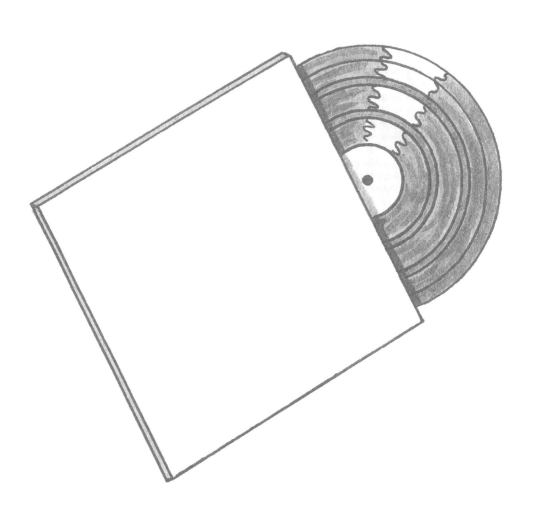

JUST BECAUSE IT RHYMES DOESN'T MEAN IT'S TRUE, WHAT SONG LIED TO YOU?

WHAT SONG IS MUCH DARKER THAN YOU REALIZED WHEN YOU FIRST HEARD IT?

....

....

....

....

....

....

....

....

....

....

....

....

....

....

....

....

....

....

....

....

NAME A MUSICAL ARTIST WHOSE FASHION SENSE YOU ADMIRE.

....

WHY?

....

....

....

....

....

....

....

....

....

....

....

....

....

....

....

....

....

Match the Color to the Song

The color doesn't need to be part of the song title,
but it could stir a feeling or create a musical memory.
Tell the story behind each.

RED

....

....

....

GREEN

....

....

....

BLUE

....

....

....

PURPLE

....

....

....

ORANGE ....
....
....

YELLOW ....
....
....

WHITE ....
....
....

BLACK ....
....
....

WHAT SONG MOST OFTEN
GETS STUCK IN YOUR HEAD? WHY?

....

....

....

....

....

....

....

....

....

....

....

....

....

....

....

....

....

....

MY MUSICAL PREJUDICES:
YOU KNOW YOU HAVE THEM, BUT WHAT ARE THEY?
WHAT GENRES DO YOU SHRINK FROM AND WHY?

....

....

....

....

....

....

....

....

....

....

....

....

....

....

....

....

....

....

....

WHAT SONGS MAKE YOUR COMMUTE GO FASTER? WHY?

WHAT'S YOUR FAVORITE
AUDIENCE PARTICIPATION SONG?

(Example: The Village People's "Y.M.C.A.,"
any song that requires clapping or call-and-response.)

Musical Geography

Make a list of cities, states, neighborhoods, and the musical memories you associate with them:

....

....

....

....

....

....

....

....

....

....

....

....

....

....

....

....

....

....

BEST USE OF A CHILDREN'S CHORUS IN MUSIC.

Think: Pink Floyd's "The Wall" or Jay-Z's
"Hard Knock Life." Defend your choice.

....

....

....

....

....

....

....

....

....

....

....

....

....

....

....

....

....

....

WHAT'S YOUR SIGNIFICANT
OTHER'S FAVORITE SONG? WHY?

....

....

....

....

....

....

....

....

....

....

....

....

....

....

....

....

....

....

....

....

....

WHAT'S YOUR FAVORITE SONG
LYRIC THAT PAINTS A PICTURE
OR SETS A SCENE? DRAW IT HERE.

WHAT SONG REPRESENTS FREEDOM FOR YOU—EITHER PERSONAL OR NATIONAL? WHY?

WHAT SONGS ARE YOU MOST LIKELY
TO SING IN THE SHOWER?

>>> Metallica wrote a song about Ernest Hemingway's *For Whom the Bell Tolls*, and Led Zeppelin has references to J.R.R. Tolkien's *Lord of the Rings* all over its songs. What are your favorite literary references in songs?

What musical genre do you wish you
appreciated more?

....

Ask your friends on social media for
recommendations. What did you learn?

....

....

....

....

....

....

....

....

....

....

....

....

....

....

....

....

WHAT SONGS ABOUT TIME
EVOKE THE MOST MEMORIES?

Examples: Cyndi Lauper's "Time After Time" or Coldplay's "Clocks."

....

....

....

....

....

....

....

....

....

....

....

....

....

....

....

....

....

....

....

DO YOU HAVE A MUSICAL IN-JOKE
WITH A LOVED ONE? EXPLAIN.

RANDOMIZER:
PUT YOUR PLAYLIST ON SHUFFLE.
WRITE DOWN ASSOCIATIONS FOR THE FIRST 5 SONGS.

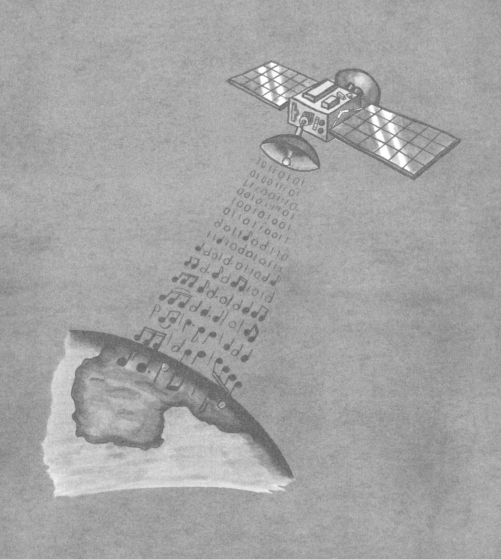

Do you have a strong memory related to it?

Create the perfect instrumental playlist:

....
....
....
....
....
....
....
....
....
....
....
....
....
....
....
....
....
....
....
....

ASSOCIATE MUSIC WITH THESE
PARTS OF YOUR HOME. EXPLAIN WHY.

KITCHEN ....
....
....

BEDROOM ....
....
....

BATHROOM ....
....
....

LIVING ROOM ....
....
....

OFFICE ....
....
....

BASEMENT ....

....

....

ATTIC ....

....

....

PORCH ....

....

....

BACK YARD ....

....

....

FRONT YARD ....

....

....

WHAT'S THE MOST MEMORABLE SONG
ABOUT THE DEVIL THAT DOESN'T INVOLVE
A FIDDLE AND A TRIP DOWN TO GEORGIA?

....

....

....

....

....

....

....

....

....

....

....

....

....

....

....

....

....

DIVINE INTERVENTION:
WHAT'S THE MOST MEMORABLE SONG THAT FEATURES OR IS ABOUT GOD?

....

....

....

....

....

....

....

....

....

....

....

....

....

....

....

....

....

....

What's the most powerful song you know that tells a story?

Why?

Who would you like to sing the story of your life? Explain
why and list some titles for this biographical album.

WHAT SONGS DO YOU WANT PLAYED AT YOUR FUNERAL? LIST AND EXPLAIN WHY.

WHICH LYRIC WOULD MAKE A FITTING EPITAPH FOR YOUR GRAVESTONE?

WHAT WOULD YOU LIKE DONE WITH THIS BOOK, ONCE YOU'VE COMPLETED IT?

....

....

....

....

....

....

....

....

....

....

....

....

....

....

....

....

....

....

READING THROUGH THE ANSWERS,
WHAT DO YOU THINK IT SAYS ABOUT YOU?

....

....

....

....

....

....

....

....

....

....

....

....

....

....

....

....

....

....

....

ROBERT K. ELDER (@robertkelder) is a tech and media executive in Chicago, and the author or editor of eight books. This book was started on a road trip to Terre Haute, Indiana, and completed on a road trip on the Blue Ridge Parkway, written on the back of tray liners from Krispy Kreme donuts. (Thanks to the employees of Krispy Kreme in Blowing Rock, North Carolina—coincidentally the hometown of author Tom Robbins.) A final draft of this book was completed in the offices of 1871 in Chicago. Visit www.robertkelder.com for more information and share your stories at www.mixtapeofmylife.com or via Twitter using @mixtapemylife.

ROB MARVIN is a writer, illustrator, and sculptor from Montana. His work has appeared in the anthology *When Animals Attack: The 70 Best Horror Films with Killer Animals,* on the horror site Dread Central, and the blogs The Montana Mancave Massacre and From Midnight with Love. www.robmarvin.com